THE UNOFFICIAL BOOK

S CLUB 7

THE UNOFFICIAL BOOK
SCLUB7

Mike Roberts

Virgin

First published in 2000 by
Virgin Books
An imprint of
Virgin Publishing Ltd
Thames Wharf Studios
Rainville Road
London
W6 9HA

A catalogue record for the book is available from the British Library.

ISBN 0 7535 0403 0

Printed and bound by Butler and Tanner Ltd, Frome and London

Designed by DW Design, London. www.dwdesign.co.uk

Contents

Join Our Club!

YOU MIGHT KNOW THE S CLUB 7 GANG **from their top-rated TV show. Or you might be a fan of their uplifting tunes and spectacular dance routines. Either way, this book will tell you everything you need to know about the boys and girls who are making a big splash all over the world!**

It may seem strange that seven high-spirited kids from Britain should find fame and fortune through a TV series set in the States, but with the appeal of MTV and the Internet, the pop world has never been smaller. The seven are well on their way to becoming the first international pop stars of the new millennium, so congratulations for being the first on your block to tune in to a gold-plated success story.

Boy or girl, brunette or blonde, upfront or off-the-wall, there's enough variety in the S Club to make sure everyone has a fave member. So what are you waiting for? Dive right in!

CHAPTER ONE

How It All Began

IT ALL STARTED WITH THE SPICE GIRLS. Having taken five unknowns to the top of the entertainment tree, superstar pop manager Simon Fuller had even bigger plans for his next project. They wouldn't just be an all-singing, all-dancing mega-successful group (as if that wasn't enough), but a fully-fledged "entertainment package" encompassing music, television and film.

When Fuller first advertised for seven young people who could act as well as sing and dance, word spread like wildfire through the acting grapevine. Cafés emptied and bars were laid bare as lines of young hopefuls formed around the block. Who would be the lucky ones groomed for superstardom? The blueprint was simple: two really good singers, two nimble dancers, someone who was really into fashion, a "cheeky kid sister" and a sensible big brother-type figure to keep an eye on them. All had to be young, talented, good looking and have the kind of personality that made them stand out from the crowd. And unlike the Spice Girls, who attracted a mostly female following, this would be a group that welcomed boys as well as girls.

There'd be something for everyone, performers and fans alike, in S Club 7. To prove it, the slogan chosen was "Everybody Is Somebody," a more inclusive version of "Girl Power." The S Club would be set up online for fans to join, and the rules were as simple as can possibly be – there was no leader, and anyone could sign up… as long as they were under the age of 23!

> There'd be something for everyone in S Club 7

S Club creator Fuller had the cash to back his dream of the perfect pop group in the shape of a rumoured large payoff, obtained after the Spice Girls had decided to break ties and manage themselves. The auditions had turned up a perfect bunch of wannabe superstars – Hannah, Jo, Rachel, Tina, Jon, Paul and Bradley – the selfsame seven you see on posters and CDs today. The first step was to fly the group out to Miami to film the 13-part TV series, after which there'd be a second series and a feature film (written by Kim Fuller, brother of Simon and the scriptwriter behind the megahit movie of 1997, *Spiceworld*). At some point an album would have to be recorded, and personal appearances, photo calls and various special events would have to be scheduled.

It was all hugely challenging for the seven – after all, actors act, dancers dance and singers sing, but here they were doing all three and jetting around the world. Previously unknown and struggling to make it in the cut-throat world of showbiz, the seven found themselves the highest of high-profile pop stars and were expected to behave as such. It was a very strange situation, not least because all their friends assumed they were rolling in cash! Truth was that the members had to exist on a small weekly allowance until profits from record sales came rolling in.

Meanwhile press and public alike would exhibit a startling hunger for details about the members of the group: what they ate for breakfast, who they were having breakfast with, and so on.

They quickly became experts in playing the fame game – like acting all cool when they were recognized in shops, and telling the occasional white lie in interviews to make themselves sound more interesting! Bradley deals with the recognition problem by wearing a floppy Kangol sun hat and glasses… Oops! We've just blown his cover. The girls might do well to adopt a disguise of their own: they stopped the traffic in Oxford Street, London's busiest shopping thoroughfare, while on a spending spree and had to be led away to sit in a room for an hour to give their fans time to disperse.

It was no coincidence whatsoever that the debut S Club single "Bring It All Back" appeared on the 7th of June. Seven was clearly going to be a major number in these guys' lives. The song quickly conquered charts and hearts to become the summer sound of 1999 in their native country, boosted by some memorable personal appearances – such as at London's Party In The Park in July, where they shared the bill with Boyzone and The Corrs. Cameras from across the globe were trained on them as they delivered a flawless performance in front of an audience which included Prince Charles. And with their single riding high in the chart, everyone knew exactly who they were.

They quickly became experts in playing the fame game

Things didn't go *quite* as smoothly when they showed up at Alton Towers theme park for another personal appearance. It had been a long journey, and Jo, Tina, Hannah and Bradley found themselves in desperate need of the bathroom. Rows of expectant fans were shocked to see their heroes emerge gingerly from their limo, only to sprint past them in the opposite direction to the stage!

Yes, even pop stars are human with the same needs and failings as the rest of us. As Paul has stressed in interviews, S Club 7 aren't robots – they're seven 17-22 year olds with all the energy, ego and insecurity that comes with growing up. But with the many different talents seven people can bring to the table, there are no limits as to what can be achieved. They know they will have to make sacrifices along the way, but they know the prize that's within their grasp is one well worth having. Having emerged in the last year of the millennium, S Club 7 aim to be the biggest stars of the new one. It's up to them to make that dream come true.

TINA

Factfile

Full Name	Tina Barrett
Nickname	Tina Bell, Teeny
Age	23
Birthdate	September 16, 1976
Birthplace	London
Starsign	Virgo
Height	5 feet 6 inches/157cm
Eyes	Brown
Likes	Fun people!
Hobbies	Playing pool, shopping
Previous jobs	Dancer
Food to die for	Anything Italian
Fave music	Puff Daddy (move over Jennifer Lopez!)

Five Things You Didn't Know About Tina:

1

The parts of her body she likes most are her oh-so-long eyelashes.

2

She describes herself as jokey, honest, sarcastic, forceful, lively and loud!

3

Her ambition is to star in a Quentin Tarantino film.

4

She prefers having a refreshing shower every morning to lazing in a bath.

5

When she was at college she never turned up for ballet classes!

CHAPTER TWO

As Seen on TV

HAVE YOU EVER THOUGHT HOW COOL IT would be to have your own television show? Hannah, Jo, Rachel, Tina, Jon, Paul and Bradley certainly did – and their dream came true with *5 Club 7 In Miami*, the TV series that launched them on a successful pop career around the world. The series was first shown in the UK (where it was known as *Miami 7*) and astounded everyone by attracting a massive 4.3 million viewers per week – a figure that made it the most popular children's show of all time. Fox Family Channel wasted no time in snapping up the show for the States and beaming it into 74 million homes. The rest, as they say, is history.

Set in the sunshine state of Florida and with an additional cast including U.S. sitcom stars, alligators and jetskis, the series stars the seven as – you guessed it! – a pop group. Their shady manager, Danny Parsons, sends them off to Miami to perform in a hotel (owned by the equally shady Howard Borlotti) after they complain they haven't been getting enough glamorous gigs back home. They expect to be living in the lap of luxury, but find a reality that's rather less appealing! Each of the thirteen episodes so far screened features fun, sunshine and a bit of adventure – and, of course, an opportunity for one or two songs.

As we've mentioned, the seven aren't the only famous faces in evidence. Manager Danny Parsons is played by Gary Whelan, an old pal of Jon's from Britain's leading soap opera *EastEnders*, while the part of Jill Ward is played by Cathy Dennis. Apart from appearing in *Beverly Hills 90210*, this talented Brit scored many a pop hit in the UK in the late 1980s and early 1990s – and indeed wrote three for the debut S Club album. So if the seven ever needed hints and tips on stardom, they didn't have far to look!

They ran into some interesting celebrities off-set, too, including Latin diva Gloria Estefan, actor Emilio Estevez and rapper Ice-T. To Jon's delight, his dream girl Cameron Diaz was sighted just down the road. It's being suggested that there'll be some very famous faces guest-starring in S Club 7's second season – so whatever you do, stay tuned.

The 18-hour-a-day filming schedule – from dawn until two in the morning on some days – was certainly challenging for the youngsters, and Jo in particular was taken aback by how little time they had to themselves. Far from having a "money for nothing" job, as some of their pals back home had joked, they were pushing themselves to the limit in take after take after take. But they came back with 13 episodes of the series in their hand luggage, so no one could say it hadn't been worth it.

Everyone enjoyed their time in Miami, though Tina has pointed out that they were based in the quiet part of town and not the "jumpin'" South Beach where it all happens. The locals got to know the gang pretty quickly and were always asking them how filming was going, which cheered up the homesick among them. Any time not taken up in front of the cameras was spent playing games of beach volleyball with the hunky locals. That came in handy for episode seven, entitled "Volleyball," in which they are set up by Howard to lose in a volleyball competition. Needless to say, they do their best to make him look an idiot… not difficult, as anyone who has seen the show will know!

In some respects, Miami was just like home – after all, there's a Burger King and McDonalds on every high street in Britain! Yet in other ways things were very different. Hannah was reminded that she was in a foreign country when she went sightseeing and had a close encounter with an alligator. She was OK sitting and watching, but when it opened its jaws and came straight for her she was up and gone quicker than you can say S Club!

It's reckoned by those involved in the TV show that the seven managed to wear over 120 costumes between them in the course of filming – that's 17 each! – and sing 15 different songs. Shooting took 13 weeks, and Paul turned 22 during their Miami stay. Any excuse for an S Club Party!

Though life's little luxuries were generally cheaper in Miami than their native Britain, not all the S Clubbers found things totally to their liking. Jon found Miami didn't cater for vegetarians, and ended up living on salads, bread and water. But when it came to shops, the mall called the Galleria, where shopping scenes were filmed, offered over 150 different places for the girls to spend their hard-earned cash. Jo reckons the four of them spent over $300 in under an hour!

In addition to the 13 regular episodes that made up the first series, a special one-hour TV feature film called *Back To The 50s* was screened in Britain to coincide with the release of the album, attracting a huge television audience in an early Saturday night slot. Even better, it had a premiere like a real film in London's West End, and Rachel recalls looking out of their hotel window at the crowds of people waiting to get in. As she admits, the group had to pinch themselves in case they were dreaming. And, to show they can see the funny side of everything, the S Clubbers gave permission for some rib-tickling out-takes to be shown after the screening. These included one real classic – a scene when Jo and Paul crash their car in some mud. Jo kept having to spit the mud out of her mouth, and just couldn't do it!

All in all, the seven were sad to leave Fort Lauderdale, the Miami resort that had played host to them for just over three months. The hotel where they lived is called the Florida Paradise on screen, but should you be planning to take a trip to Miami you'll find it labelled on the map as Villas By The Sea. But beware and make sure you watch where you tread – a deadly rattlesnake was found in a bush near where the seven were filming, causing no end of a commotion! With animal-loving Jon in the cast, they let it go once shooting had finished. Just like S Club, it'll be back one day!

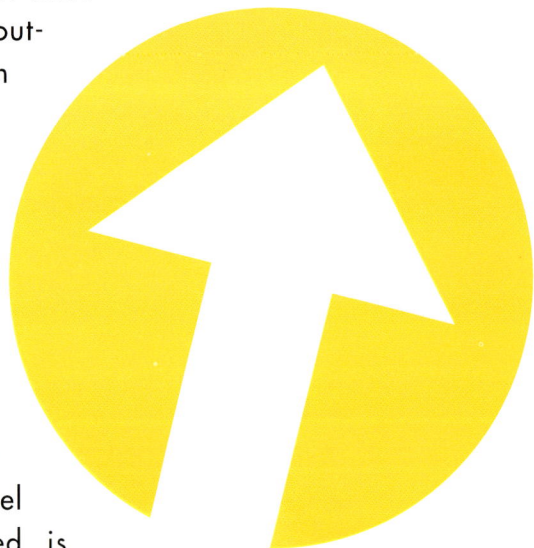

The group had to pinch themselves in case they were dreaming

Let's Get Personal:

JON

Factfile

Full Name	Jonathan Lee
Age	17
Birthdate	April 26, 1982
Birthplace	Croydon
Starsign	Taurus
Height	5 feet 7 inches/170cm
Eyes	Hazel
Likes	Robin Williams
Hobbies	Computer games, reading
Previous jobs	Actor
Food to die for	Vegetarian
Fave music	Anything!

Five Things You Didn't Know About Jon:

1

His fave parts of his body are his earlobes, because they're not too big and not too small.

2

He describes himself as confident, focused, ambitious, fun-loving, outgoing, sarcastic and funny!

3

His ambition is to explore the Great Barrier Reef.

4

He once operated the lift for fellow guests in an Italian hotel dressed only in his underwear!

5

While at school, he irritated teachers by copying their mannerisms.

CHAPTER THREE

On Our Way!

TAKE ANY SEVEN INDIVIDUALS UNDER THE age of 23 off the street and you'd probably find a mixture of backgrounds, and S Club 7 are no different. There's a high proportion of natural performers in the group – kids who had star quality at a time most of us were still taking our first steps – but that doesn't mean this gang have their heads in a parallel showbiz universe. Far from it!

Hannah was brought up in Great Yarmouth, a sleepy English seaside resort. She had to make the move to the big city, London, to realize her dreams. Having played her first stage role at three, she landed a part in the National Youth Musical Theatre's production of *Pendragon* and was appearing in London's West End as a cast member of *Bugsy Malone* when the S Club call came.

If she hadn't managed to make it in showbiz, Hannah wouldn't have minded being a nurse, a professional tennis player or a fitness instructor. She's still a small-town girl at heart and regularly returns to Great Yarmouth to look up family and friends. She worked at a holiday camp there before the acting bug bit, making her ideally suited for fun by the sea in Miami, but remembers her youth more for the fact that she broke her leg, arm, toe and finger… at different times, of course! The other thing that takes her back is best friend Sheridan Smith, who's like a

> **Jo's first professional singing job was at the age of just 12**

second sister to her (she's already got an older sis and a brother). Of course, now that she's in S Club there's no shortage of female advice to be had – whether she asks for it or not! Something else worth mentioning is that there are more websites devoted to her on the Net than the rest of the group members put together.

Jon might be the youngest, but he was certainly the best known before joining the S Club. He graduated from the famous Sylvia Young Theatre School in London (fellow past pupils include Emma "Baby Spice" Bunton) and soon became an up-and-coming TV star, playing the part of Josh in the UK soap opera *EastEnders*.

Before that Jon had acted in a TV film called *Mill On The Floss*, and had appeared on stage in the title role of *Oliver!* at the London Palladium. He claims he auditioned for this off the street, having appeared in school plays from the age of four and worked with a local drama group. And as he's as stubborn as his star sign, Taurus the bull, we're not going to argue!

His best friends and unofficial fan club are older brothers Jamie and Dan, who go everywhere with him when he's not on pop star duty. Jon once entered a talent competition which Bradley's record-producer father was judging; little did the pair guess they'd end up in a band together.

Brad's dad may have been a successful musician with reggae group The Cool Notes, but there were no early signs that the young Londoner would be following in his parental footsteps. His pre-fame jobs included selling replacement windows and working at burger and pizza restaurants.

The one thing he did inherit was a love of the night-time. Given the choice (which he isn't too often these days!), night owl Bradley would be happy to wake at midday and take it from there. By the evening he's the life and soul of the party, and is always the last to turn in after a hard night's clubbing.

On Our Way!

Blonde bombshell Jo O'Meara had been spotted singing country and western music in a restaurant. She had already had a Top 40 hit single in Germany, and clearly had the star quality needed to become a fully-fledged teen star. Just as well really – this headstrong miss left school without taking any of her exams, a course of action which is certainly not recommended!

Jo's first professional singing job was at the age of just 12, after her father encouraged her to sing "The Locomotion" at a local karaoke night. By the time someone finally unplugged the machine from the wall she'd determined her chosen career, but making a living from music wasn't always easy. Jobs in a supermarket and pet store paid the way until she got her C&W crooning break and – eventually – an audition for S Club 7.

Paul had certainly packed a lot into his young life before S Club 7 – his previous jobs included delivering mail and leaflets, collecting refuse, working in an office and doing security at a nightclub! He was keen to make it in show business any which way he could, and had been in a number of rock bands who had nearly made it. Some of the friends he made in his rock days are providing the accompaniment to some well-known stars these days, so if he hadn't grabbed a piece of the spotlight you might've seen the gifted Mr Cattermole playing along in the background with someone else.

Paul had a good role model on his musical route to stardom. His great-grandfather was the managing director of Abbey Road studios in London, where the Beatles and many other legendary pop groups recorded. On the other side of the family, his grandfather was a particle physicist, and Paul claims to have been one of the few people to enjoy physics at school.

Rachel admits she gets butterflies every time she sets foot on stage

Rachel Stevens is an ambitious Aries who worked in films and fashion before bringing her talents to S Club 7. With a model's looks, she's keen to stay picture-perfect, and consequently you'll never see her looking as if she's just got out of bed. She knows her footwear, too, having worked in a shoe store before bigger things came calling. She comes from a large family, and with three brothers ready to step in she never has trouble repelling unwanted admirers. She and her boyfriend have been dating for three years, so don't get your hopes up just yet.

Dance-crazy Tina has always paid great attention to her feet, but she didn't think she'd end up working for a foot doctor. Luckily her job as receptionist meant she kept well away from any less-than-pleasant sights and smells, but she's delighted she doesn't have to book bunion-sufferers' appointments any more. Her dance to fame began at the age of three when she started ballet classes and, two years later, had learned enough to appear in the pantomime *Cinderella* with British showbiz legend Lionel Blair.

It was a proud moment for S Club 7 when they were asked to appear on *Top Of The Pops*, Britain's prime-time TV showcase for pop music. Having grown up with it in their living rooms every Thursday, the seven were understandably awed by the prospect of going in front of the cameras. Rachel, in particular, admits she gets butterflies every time she has to set foot on stage, but Tina was quite at home there. She'd worked there before as a dancer, and remembered watching Mariah Carey recording her spot.

We've seen them on TV, heard them sing and read about them in magazines, but do we know who S Club 7 really are? The answer is yes – sort of. The television characters they play are based loosely on their own personalities, but with certain things exaggerated. They've all reached our television screens by very different routes, and though they get on each other's nerves at times they are generally a happy-go-lucky bunch. From the pizza parlour to the showbiz fast lane, these guys have come a long way, and there's lots more to come!

HANNAH

Factfile

Full Name	Hannah Louise Spearritt
Nicknames	Ted, Titch, Minty
Age	18
Birthdate	April 1, 1981
Birthplace	Great Yarmouth, Norfolk
Starsign	Aries
Height	5 feet 4 inches/162cm
Eyes	Blue
Likes	Leo DiCaprio and parties
Hobbies	Tennis, swimming, running
Previous jobs	Working in a holiday camp, acting
Food to die for	Sausages, turkey, potatoes and cranberry sauce!
Fave music	TLC, Faithless and Brandy

Five Things You Didn't Know About Hannah:

1

Her worst habit is pinching guys' butts – she even pinched Bradley's before they were introduced!

2

She describes herself as down-to-earth, independent, cheeky, outgoing, embarrassing, happy and chatty!

3

Her ambition is to go skiing.

4

She once threw a pot of paint at the classroom wall at school.

5

She named her treasured teddy bear, Little Ted, after her dad, who strangely enough is Big Ted!

CHAPTER FOUR

The ABC of S Club 7

TAKE AN ALPHABETICAL LOOK AT THE HOTTEST thing to come out of Britain since the Spice Girls!

A is for Attitude and Ability, which these guys (and gals) have in abundance,
Album – if you haven't heard it yet, why not?
and Abba, the biggest boy/girl group in the world – at least until S Club came along!

B stands for Bradley, the Romeo of the group, who can charm the birds from the trees, or so he claims,
"Bring It All Back," the smash hit single that announced S Club 7's arrival on the UK pop scene,
and Boring, which Jon allegedly said he thought Tina was going to be when he first met her. How wrong he was!

C can only stand for Clothes, Rachel's obsession. She won't go out looking scruffy, and even her underwear has to match,
Charts, and hearts, where the S Clubbers have taken up residence,
and CDs – millions of them!

D means Designer labels, top of Rachel's shopping list every time,
Drums, Bradley's first instrument (the neighbours complained!),
and Dogs. Jon talks to his – she's called Molly.

E means Extrovert, a word you could apply to at least six of the seven
Excitement, what we feel when we hear their music,
and *EastEnders*, the British television programme with 11 million viewers that gave Jon his first taste of fame.

F Fit, Fresh and Funky – three very appropriate adjectives where the S Club are concerned,
Fuller, boss man Simon whose idea this all was,
and Flirting, something Bradley admits he's a past master at. Look out, girls!

G stands for Geography, Paul's best subject at school – he used to read about all the places he's visiting now,
Glamour, which (sort of) rhymes with Hannah (though some would argue it describes Rachel better),
and Girlfriend, a role all the boys out there would like to audition the female S Clubbers for!

H is for Hannah, the sauciest of the group,
Heels, which she never bothers to wear (so people say "aren't you small?"),
and Hair, Jon's big obsession. You wouldn't believe the number of shampoo bottles he's got in his bathroom!

I means Individual, a label that could be applied to all the S Clubbers – no clones here!
Inspiration, the extra added ingredient they put into everything they do that raises it from ordinary to special,
and Independence, something that's very important to Hannah.

J is for Jo and Jon (what a difference a letter makes!)
JP, S Club slang for jacket potatoes, their fave microwave meal,
and (Michael) Jackson, the King of Pop and a hero to Jo.

K King, something Paul would like to be (for a day, at least!)
Kids – Bradley's baby stepsister makes his fellow S Clubbers go all gooey!
and Karaoke, the singing craze even S Clubbers can't resist.

L means London, home for our fave group and the place where the S Club story started back in 1998,
Lake District, the scenic area of England where Hannah likes to spend her holidays,
and Loneliness, which can strike even an S Clubber from time to time. Luckily there's six friendly faces just around the corner!

M is for Mobile phone, which is the best way to keep in touch with an S Clubber these days – they never stay still for long!
Miami, the sunny city where the television series we know and love came together,
and Music, the whole point of the S Club exercise.

N Naughty (but nice) is how Hannah would like to see herself,
Naked, which is how Paul sleeps when the nights are hot,
and Nerd. Tina isn't quite that bad, but she does love computers. Bill Gates is her hero!

O might mean 'Orrible, something Jo allegedly thought Tina was when they first met – but she's "actually lovely."
Optimist, something Bradley claims to be – and he's got the smile to prove it,
and Omelette, another culinary fave when time's short and a good night out beckons.

P is for Peppermint green, like the walls of Jon's bedroom at home,
Paul, a name to remember, even though he'd rather have a more interesting one,
and Pets – Jon and Bradley love dogs best, while Hannah makes do with a stuffed one called Snoop.

Q is for the Queen of England. We don't know if she's a fan, but if you bump into her, let us know!
Quiet, something you might think applies to Jon until he gets to know you,
and Quality, something that runs through everything S Club 7 do.

R means Recording studio, the place S Club 7 call a second home these days,
Romford, a town in Essex, England, where Jo is proud to hail from,
and Romance, something Hannah's put on the back burner for now. Her job comes first!

S S is for Shoes – did you know former professional dancer Tina owns no fewer than 40 pairs?
Shopping, Rachel's fave off-stage occupation. When it comes to exercising the charge card, there's no one better!
And last but not least comes S Club. What does it stand for? According to who you ask, it's Sexy (Jo), Sassy (Paul), Stupid (Hannah) or Sausages (Jon)!

T must mean Television, the way we all got to meet S Club 7 and take them to our hearts,
Travel, something they've done a lot of over the past year – just look at those luggage labels!
and TLC, Hannah's fave girl band. They're mega, she says – and who'd dare argue?

U stands for Ugly, something Paul claims he thought he was once – he's got more confidence these days, though!

Unusual, which S Club 7 most certainly are – in fact, their four girl/three boy combination makes them Unique!

and Ups and Downs, through which the seven S Clubbers always stick together.

V is for Vegetarian, which describes meat-free Jon to a T (or should that be V?),

Vibrant and Vital, both undoubted S Club attributes,

and Vain, the word many would use to describe Rachel's TV character (where's that mirror gone?).

W Wet, a state S Club often found themselves in while filming in Miami,

Waiter, which Bradley was before fame came calling,

and Wine Bar, where Jo used to perform once upon a time in her pre-fame days.

X   X-ceptional, the only way to describe the S Club 7 album that contains all their hits and much more

X-files – Paul's strange dream of being chased by killer bees would definitely be a case for Mulder and Scully,

and X-tra cheese on that pizza, please, Bradley (no, they'll never let him forget his old job!).

Y   Young, free and single – a description that fits our S Clubbers down to the ground!

Yuk, the sound Bradley made when he found a spider sitting in his face cream,

and Yikes! That's the sound Jo made when she acquired her famous barbed-wire tattoo. The pain's gone now, thankfully.

Z   could be for Zoo, a fave day out for animal lover Jon,

Zany, Paul's wit – an acquired taste, say some of his band-mates!

and "ZZZZZZ," the sound you'll hear after a long hard day's filming. It's tiring work being a pop star, you know!

Let's Get Personal:

BRADLEY

Factfile

Full Name	Bradley John McIntosh
Age	18
Birthdate	August 8, 1981
Birthplace	London
Starsign	Leo
Height	5 feet 6 inches/157cm
Eyes	Brown
Likes	Sport, hanging out at Burger King
Hobbies	Computer games
Previous jobs	Working at Pizza Hut and Burger King, selling windows and doors
Food to die for	Jamaican
Fave music	Reggae, R&B

Five Things You Didn't Know About Bradley:

1
His fave part of his body is his head.

2
He describes himself as positive, confident, crazy, kind, a joker, handsome and gorgeous!

3
His ambition is to fly.

4
He enjoys dangerous theme-park rides, but can only manage two before throwing up!

5
He was always getting into trouble at school for playing practical jokes on the teachers.

CHAPTER FIVE

Pure Pop – With An Edge!

A MAJOR PART OF THE S CLUB 7 RECIPE for international megastardom is their irresistible music. In between basking on the beaches of Florida filming the first TV series, S Club 7 were recording their debut album, *S Club*. With songs written by the platinum team behind the Spice Girls, plus Simon Fuller protégés the Dufflebag Boys, and a telling contribution from the S Clubbers themselves, it would prove a major success, more than living up to the record company's description: "pure pop – with an edge!"

The first step was to make a mark on the UK singles chart. Released on 7 June 1999, "Bring It All Back" was an uptempo, upbeat and optimistic song reminiscent of "I Want You Back," an early hit for Michael Jackson and his brothers. A song *that* catchy stood every chance of doing well, except for the fact that it was up against a heavyweight challenger. No less a pop icon than Madonna was set to release a new single the very same week. Who was going to win?

It looked dark for a moment, but when the sales figures came in there were seven sighs of relief when "Bring It All Back" entered the UK charts at the very top. It was a proud moment for them all, not least because they got a

quarter of the writing credits on the song. The following week brought the award of a silver disc for 200,000 copies sold, which made up for the disappointment of being deposed from number one – but even then they stayed above new entrants Britney Spears and 'N Sync. The single would stay in the UK Top 40 all summer long.

Come the end of September, summer had well and truly disappeared and it was time for another single to warm the fans as the leaves were falling. As you'd guess from the name, "S Club Party" wasn't just a single – it was a party anthem! Into the chart it shot, debuting at number two with a bullet. And, just like the first time, Britney was left floundering in S Club's wake, as was country diva Shania Twain. The song would stick around in the top three for another fortnight, brightening the airwaves with its infectious chorus and rap-style verses. S Club 7 had arrived – and they certainly weren't one-hit wonders!

Ms. Twain had her revenge in October when the S Clubbers' first album arrived on the racks. Having amassed 64 weeks on the chart, the Canadian's *Come On Over* refused to *move* over. But it didn't matter, for the end of the month brought another disc for the Clubbers' wall – gold this time, as 100,000 copies of the record had passed across the counter in a matter of days. Soon they'd received a Platinum disc too, as CD sales reached 300,000 copies.

So what was it about *S Club* that made it *the* album to be seen with that summer? Certainly the packaging was perfect, with beachside scenes and pin-up pictures of the guys and girls to set fans swooning – but if truth be told it was what was in the grooves that made this 11-song package the hottest around. The album could only really have kicked off with "Bring It All Back," most people's introduction to the S Club sound and the song the group members had helped write themselves.

Next comes "You're My Number One" – one of two tracks on the album penned by the Dufflebag Boys songwriting and production team, and a song first heard in the "Volleyball"

episode of the TV series. Like the game itself, the super-energetic music is guaranteed to leave you out of breath.

After such danceable beginnings it's time for a change of pace, provided by a breathtaking ballad, "Two In A Million." This had featured strongly in episode five of the television series, the one where the group thought a record company boss had come to stay at the hotel. Such was the public reaction to the song that it was selected as the third British single, which narrowly missed out on the Christmas number one spot.

The album could only really have kicked off with "Bring It All Back"

Next up on the playlist is "S Club Party," the singalong second single that namechecks each S Clubber in turn and proved to be one of the year's party anthems. Then there's "Everybody Wants You" (which you may recall from the hurricane-hit episode four of the series), swiftly followed by "Viva La Fiesta." This salsa-style song was co-written by Cathy Dennis, who also lent a hand with "Two In A Million" and appeared in the TV series as Jill Ward.

Heard most memorably in the final show of the first season, "Gonna Change The World" features the boys singing. It offers the very pertinent message that if you want to change the world you have to start with yourself. Talking of getting personal, the following track "I Really Miss You" does just that, and is doubtless dedicated to absent boy/girlfriends by Rachel and Paul – and their families by everyone else!

As its title suggests, "Friday Night" invites you to enjoy yourself in true S Club style. It's a funky slice of R&B that managed to escape being featured on television and is one of Rachel's favourite album tracks. "It's A Feel Good Thing" keeps the party mood going, and boasts something unusual – a subtitle, "Buenos Tiempo." Whether this is a nod to Miami and its Hispanic population we don't know, but good times are guaranteed as the Dufflebag Boys pack this one out with hooks and beats a-plenty. This one was first heard in the very first episode of the series, if anyone can remember back that far! Last but far from least comes "Hope For The Future," the third and last Cathy Dennis song of the collection and a forward-looking way to end the album.

While the songs they release have all been specially written for them, the TV series also saw the seven tackle classics from Abba, the Beatles and others. Though the group's contribution to the first album was small in songwriting terms, sources claim that future releases will see their ratio of credits rise to between 20 and 40 percent – and that was confirmed when Universal Music signed up the publishing rights to their songs in the face of tough competition. Expect to hear more of their own individual musical tastes coming through in future releases – Jon, for instance, is a major Backstreet Boys fan (though we hear he also listens to The Corrs), while Bradley would just *love* to get a bit more dancefloor into the mixes!

All these possible changes would just be improving on perfection, however, because the S Club brand of pop has already proved popular the world over. "Bring It All Back" reached the Top 20 in Australia and Denmark and topped the charts in New Zealand, where Jo has a lot of family (maybe they all bought a copy!). Hopefully it will give her a chance to look them up sometime soon!

The S Club brand of pop has already proved popular the world over

46

Pure Pop – With An Edge!

In November 1999, S Club 7 took part in *Abbamania*, a tribute album dedicated to the Swedish Eurovision winners. "Dancing Queen," a number one hit in 1976, was their choice – not surprisingly, really, since they'd already performed it in episode 11 of the TV series. They were joined in saluting the super Swedes by Westlife, Steps, The Corrs, B*Witched, Boyzone's Stephen Gately and others. Next up was a new single, the aforementioned "Two In A Million," released on December 13, 1999, while the group's first ever commercially available video, *It's An S Club Thing*, was unveiled in the UK on November 22. Meanwhile the S Club plan for world domination had begun in earnest with the release of "Bring It All Back" in the USA. Would they repeat the success they had already achieved in their home country? Only time would tell. One thing was already certain – it was going to be a music-packed millennium for S Club fans.

RACHEL

Factfile

Full Name	Rachel Stevens
Nickname	Rach
Age	21
Birthdate	April 9, 1978
Birthplace	London
Starsign	Aries
Height	5 feet 3 inches/160cm
Eyes	Dark brown
Likes	Matthew McConaughey, the smell of fresh bread
Hobbies	Pets, football
Previous jobs	Model, working for a shoe store, film company and fashion company
Food to die for	Baked beans on toast
Fave music	R&B, Backstreet Boys

Five Things You Didn't Know About Rachel:

1

She claims her fave part of her body is her stomach, because of her belly button ring.

2

She describes herself as sensitive, caring, a good friend, honest, ambitious, confident and funny!

3

While filming in Miami, Rachel shipped the entire contents of her wardrobe out to the hotel!

4

She's always wanted her legs to be a teeny bit longer.

5

Her mobile phone bill is equivalent to NASA's yearly budget (allegedly!).

CHAPTER SIX

Seven On Seven

PUT SEVEN VERY DIFFERENT people together and it's impossible to say how they'll interact. Put them on a stage and if they've got talent they can play the pop star role, but who knows what'll happen once the curtain closes? How will they get on? Can they stand the sight of each other? And will World War III break out at the end of a fifteen-hour TV shoot when they make that mad dash to the hotel?

Happily, after the odd moment of uncertainty, the S Club story has got off to a stupendous start. Socially they split into groups which change by the day, and all make a point of keeping in touch with their existing pals. As all have showbiz backgrounds, they are only too aware of the pitfalls of fame, and have adjusted well to the breakneck schedule they have had to meet so far.

The seven all live separately, four of them with their parents. The homes of the independent trio range from Hannah's tiny rented apartment in north London, to a two-bedroom apartment in hip west London

Romance between the group members is definitely out of the question

bought for Tina by her property developer dad. Living separately is a conscious decision to give themselves space, although filming in Miami thrust them all together for weeks on end – with unpredictable results! Jon reckons they'd end up killing each other if they had to do that back home. He has recalled that each night he'd walk into his own hotel room, shut the door behind him and let out his feelings with a loud, long scream!

None of the S Club members were great friends before they joined the group. Paul and Hannah both knew each other as they'd starred in a stage show together, while Jon and Bradley knew each other by sight, but that was about it.

It's been reported that things took time to settle down between Tina and Jo, by common agreement the loudest, most outspoken members of the band. They've managed to bury the hatchet, and now they natter away like "a couple of old women," or so Jon claims! If it's in the best interests of the group, they'll happily put their differences aside because S Club 7 comes first and foremost! Now they're the best of friends.

Romance between the group members is definitely out of the question ("it would be like kissing your brother or sister," one has said) but Paul and Hannah have been linked by the British press in the past, which amused Paul, if not his girlfriend of three years! Hannah, in her turn, had made it clear she was interested in Scott from Five, but when the two got together it was friendship, not love, that resulted.

Paul, as the "elder statesman" of the seven, is the one who's most confident about his looks, and thinks some of the others – Rachel especially – shouldn't be so insecure. He even laughs about his unusual surname, Cattermole. Tina isn't alone among the seven in respecting his professionalism, and the fact

that he will put in 100 percent effort even at the end of an exhausting day. She does admit that his sarcastic wit can take a bit of getting used to. She reckons he acts as if he thinks he knows everything – which of course he doesn't. She does!

Hannah is bubbly and fun, but she's also a very private person who often keeps things to herself. If she's having a bad time, then the reasons have to be teased out of her. You get the feeling that if S Club 7 ended for whatever reason (not that it's likely to anytime soon) she'd happily return to Great Yarmouth and pick up where she left off.

Jo reckons she's the softest and soppiest of the whole group, and is keen to tell anyone who listens that despite her tattoos and body piercings she's far from the hard case she's sometimes taken to be. Bradley can see past the surface to the real Jo, and likes her bubbly character. He warns, though, that Jo can get a little on the moody side when the days are long and the workload is hard. But then, don't we all?

Rachel is rather different than her television personality. Far from running around checking her make-up, she's pretty relaxed – so much so that Jon once described her and her boyfriend as "Mr & Mrs Nice"! She's always asking her fellow S Clubbers if they're all right, which she admits gets on their nerves a bit, but this is one caring, sharing person. She admits she gets lonely even when she's with the other six, so her mobile phone bills have to be seen to be believed!

Tina admits she has a temper on her, but happily you won't see it too often. She's content to go with the flow and ignore little everyday annoyances. She has the ability to drift into her own little world, where no one and nothing can put a frown on her face. There's a point, though, where she'll let you know exactly what's on her mind – so practical jokers like Brad had better beware!

Bradley and Jon are most likely to come to blows over timekeeping. For Jon, being punctual is one of the most important things in life – it shows respect, and respect for everything, be it human or animal, is number one on his list of priorities. Brad, on the other hand, is unlikely to show up anywhere at the appointed time – it's just his way. He's probably stuck somewhere chatting on his mobile, and there's a ten to one chance it's a lady on the other end!

Where most pop people put on a show the moment the spotlight comes on, like Robbie Williams, Bradley is the exact opposite. Maybe it's the fact that he avoided the traditional route to fame, but he's a very natural person who does exactly what his instincts tell him to. A notorious party animal when he's with his pals, he's the quietest S Clubber by far on stage. Catch him on his own in a quiet moment and you'll be lucky to get two words out of him.

Speaking of words, did you know that S Club 7 have their own secret language? It's true! Put your ear to the dressing-room door and you might hear some very strange things indeed. If you're male and you hear yourself described as "so Leo" by one of the girls, then you're in luck – they fancy you! (The Leo in question is, of course, a certain Mr DiCaprio.) "Deets" are details, "Boglins" are children and "Chickster" a girl the fellas would like to get to know better.

So, S Club 7 – fast friends or envious enemies? As Jon has remarked, if you'd told him he was going to be thrown in with six total strangers and they'd have a hit single, he'd have told you not to be so stupid. But he was, they did and it happened, and everything's just fine. Besides, if two members ever have a row, there are still five friendly faces to confide in!

Let's Get Personal:

PAUL

Factfile

Full Name	Paul Cattermole
Nickname	Guacamole
Age	22
Birthdate	March 7, 1977
Birthplace	St Albans, Hertfordshire
Starsign	Pisces
Height	5 feet 9 inches/176cm
Eyes	Brown
Likes	Robert De Niro and Sandra Bullock
Hobbies	Partying, playing guitar
Previous jobs	Working behind a bar, delivering mail, doorman
Food to die for	Whole grilled chicken
Fave music	Anything with a beat

Five Things You Didn't Know About Paul:

1

His fave parts of his body are his snake-like hips.

2

He describes himself as sensitive, loud, funny, philosophical, easy-going and sarcastic!

3

He never cleans the bathroom because he says it's there to be used, not cleaned!

4

He has a habit of sucking his thumb when tired or stressed.

5

When he was young, he was known to go sleepwalking at the dead of night with no clothes on!

CHAPTER SEVEN

Catch Ya Later!

SO WHAT DOES THE FUTURE HOLD FOR S Club 7? Well, things have definitely taken a turn for the better since, when they arrived at the Cannes Film Festival early in 1999 to promote their television series, the group were described in the French newspapers as "the Spice Girls with their male dancers"! Now, of course, S Club 7 are well known in their own right. And the chances are that the new millennium will be even kinder to them as they sweep all before them with their own distinctive brand of pop.

The challenge they face is to maintain the impact they've had and extend the S Club kingdom throughout the world – nothing less than stardom on a global scale is acceptable! The Spices have already done it, of course, and since the seven are being guided by the man who wrote the book and sold the T-shirt Spicewise, don't be surprised to see a similar thing happen for his new charges in 2000, 2001 and beyond.

The year it all started, 1999, ended in spectacular style as S Club 7 played the *Smash Hits* Poll Winners Party in December, an annual show where the awards are voted for by the readers of Britain's top teen magazine. The fact that the S Club were selected to perform alongside the likes of B*witched, Steps and Five proved they had already reached amazing heights in the pop stratosphere, especially

since each and every one of the acts chosen had registered at least one Top 5 hit during the year. S Club 7, of course, had had two!

A keen soap opera fan, Jon had to set his video recorder to catch all the shows he'd miss as the S Clubbers waved goodbye to home and family and set off on a three-month tour. They were to visit all the countries where the TV series is shown: Tina was dying to see Japan again, having celebrated her 21st birthday there, while Jo set her sights on Egypt and the Pyramids. Not that there'd be much time for sightseeing as the group's itinerary included visits to radio stations, TV channels and record stores, plus some live concerts. Luckily all seven know they have to put in the work to reap the rewards, so with any luck they'll all stay the course. If anyone left, would they be replaced? We guess they'd have to be unless the seven suddenly turned into S Club 6! Not that we think it'll happen, mind you.

If there's one thing the S Clubbers have yet to crack, it's playing their music live. But that's about to change. Once musicians have been hired and rehearsed, a set of songs selected and those important costume changes organized, expect the S Club 7 live experience to come your way late in 2000.

A range of designer clothes is also part of the S Club plan, with each member contributing fashion ideas. Can

> **Tina was dying to see Japan again, having celebrated her 21st birthday there**

you imagine Tina tank tops, Hannah hipsters or Bradley boots? The S Club logo lends itself to many kinds of fashion statements – and with seven very different styles to mix and match you'd be spoiled for choice!

Of more immediate importance at the moment is the filming of the second series of the television show in Los Angeles, a long way from the cold, wet British winter. When *S Club 7 in LA* is shown around the world later in 2000 it's sure to help the S Club climb even further up the ladder of superstardom.

There are single releases galore planned for the States, another album is tentatively scheduled for late 2000, while script work on a feature film is already under way. Success for the movie could well see the seven stars considering individual careers away from music and away from the group.

Will this mean the end of the Club, or could they be the biggest musical phenomenon of the new millennium? Only time will tell, but we (and they) are going to have fun finding out!

JO

Factfile

Full Name	Joanne Velda O'Meara
Age	20
Birthdate	April 29, 1979
Birthplace	Romford, Essex
Starsign	Taurus
Height	5 feet 4 Inches/162cm
Eyes	Blue
Likes	Her dog Pepsi, guys with a sense of fun
Hobbies	singing karaoke
Previous jobs	Worked in a pet store and a supermarket and was a singer in a restaurant
Food to die for	Sausage and egg muffin, steak
Fave music	R&B – every time!

Five Things You Didn't Know About Jo:

1
She claims her fave part of her body is her stomach because she's recently lost weight.

2
She describes herself as loud, generous, brave, determined, caring and moody!

3
She cried buckets when she saw the last episode of the TV show's first series because of all the memories it brought back.

4
She eats too much chocolate, and once ate five bars one after the other.

5
Her ambitions are to learn another language and to visit the pyramids in Egypt.